Andrew Brodie Basics

LET'S DO HANDWRITING

FOR AGES 10-11

with over **100** reward stickers

- Structured practice of handwriting strokes
- Extra tips on style and tidiness
- Regular progress checks

Published 2014 by Bloomsbury Publishing Plc
50 Bedford Square, London, WC1B 3DP
29 Earlsfort Terrace, Dublin 2, Ireland

www.bloomsbury.com

Bloomsbury is a registered trade mark of Bloomsbury Publishing Plc

ISBN 978-14729-1028-8

First published 2014
© 2014 Andrew Brodie
Cover and inside illustrations of Martha the Meerkat and Andrew Brodie © 2014 Nikalas Catlow
Other inside illustrations © 2014 Steve Evans

A CIP catalogue for this book is available from the British Library.

10 9 8 7 6 5 4 3 2

Printed in China by Leo Paper Products

MIX
Paper from responsible sources
FSC® C020056
www.fsc.org

To see our full range of titles visit **www.bloomsbury.com**

BLOOMSBURY

Notes for parents

What's in this book

This is the sixth in the series of *Andrew Brodie Basics: Let's Do Handwriting* books. Each book features a clearly structured approach to developing and improving children's handwriting, an essential skill for correct spelling and effective written communication. Check the handwriting style used at your child's school as there are slight variations between schools. The style used in this book reflects the most popular one.

The National Curriculum states that, during the later part of Key Stage 2, children should 'write legibly, fluently and with increasing speed'. They need to choose which shape of letter to use and whether or not to join specific letters. They should also practise an unjoined style, perhaps for labelling diagrams, and capital letters, for filling in forms or writing clear addresses. Working their way through this book will help your child to achieve these skills.

How you can help

Make sure your child is ready for their handwriting practice. They should be able to place this book flat on a desk or table; make sure that their chair and table are of appropriate heights so that they are comfortable and can reach their work easily. Check that the work area is well-lit with clear, uncluttered space.

Your child should hold the book at an appropriate angle so that their handwriting is clearly visible to them. If your child is left-handed, the book will need to be turned to the opposite angle to that used by right-handed people: it is essential that they can see their work, rather than covering it with their hand as they write.

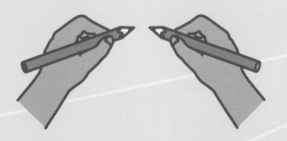

Martha the Meerkat

Look out for Martha the Meerkat, who tells your child what to focus on ready for the progress check at the end of each section.

Andrew Brodie says…

On some pages there are further tips and reminders from Andrew Brodie, which are devised to encourage your child to self-check their work.

When your child does well, makes sure you tell them so! The colourful stickers in the middle of this book can be a great reward for good work and a big incentive for future progress.

The answer section

The answer section at the back of this book can be a useful teaching tool: ask your child to compare their handwriting to the exemplars shown on the progress check answer pages. If they have written their letters and words correctly, congratulate them, but if they haven't, don't let them worry about it! Instead, encourage them to learn the correct versions. Give lots of praise for any success.

Practise unjoined letters

Unjoined letters can be useful for labelling diagrams.

Notice that all of these letters are formed in a similar way. They all start like a letter c.

Here is a different way of writing letter g, using a loop.

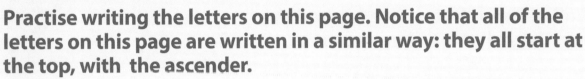

Practise writing the letters on this page. Notice that all of the letters on this page are written in a similar way: they all start at the top, with the ascender.

Practising unjoined letters helps for when we join them.

Andrew Brodie says...

Most of the letters on this page have ascenders but letter **p** has a descender.

4

Practise unjoined letters

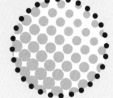

Unjoined letters can be useful for words on posters.

Practise writing the letters on this page.

Here is a different letter j and a different letter y, each of which has a loop.

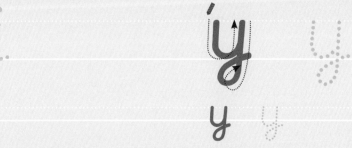

Practise letter e

Practise writing the letters on this page.

Unjoined letters can be useful for writing email addresses.

 v v v

 w w w

e e e

f f f f

s s s s

x x x x

z z z z

Special forms of letters

This type of letter **x** can be very useful for algebra.

Look carefully at this letter x. Can you copy it exactly?

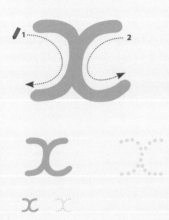

Now look at these special forms of letters f and z. Some people like to use these as they are easier to join from.

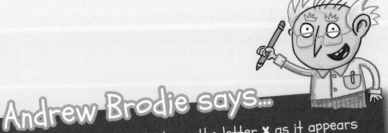

Andrew Brodie says...

It is really important to learn the letter **x** as it appears on this page because you will use it in your algebra work in maths. It's very easy when you get used to it, and it joins well to other letters.

Write the alphabet using unjoined letters.

a b c d e f g h i j k l m n o p q r s t u v w x y z

Time taken, in seconds.

Write the alphabet again. Time yourself. How quickly can you write it?

Try writing the alphabet again. Can you write it even more quickly and still keep it tidy?

Now try it on a wavy line, as fast as you can.

How quickly can you write the algebraic letter x? Write five neat copies of the large one and ten neat copies of the small one.

Write the alphabet backwards! Time yourself. How quickly can you write it?

Practise capital letters

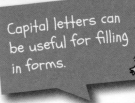

Practise writing the letters on this page.

A A

B B

C C

D D

E E

F F

G G

H H

I I

J J

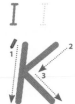

K K

L L

M M

Practise writing the letters on this page.

N N N N
N N N

P P P
P P P

R R R
R R R

T T T
T T T

V V V
V V V

X X X
X X X

Z Z Z
Z Z Z

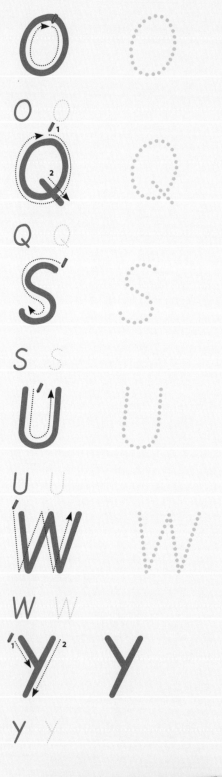

O O O
O O O

Q Q Q
Q Q Q

S S S
S S S

U U U
U U U

W W W
W W W

Y Y Y
Y Y Y

Capital letters are useful for writing addresses.

Practise capital letters

Letters are arranged in a special way on a computer keyboard, to make typing easier. This is known as the QWERTY keyboard because of the order of the first six letters. Copy the blank letters onto the QWERTY keyboard below, writing every letter very clearly.

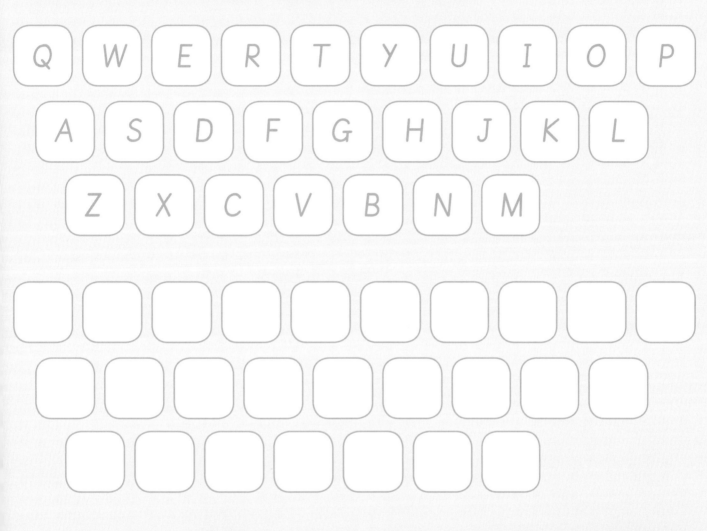

Andrew Brodie says...

Knowing the layout of a computer keyboard will help you type more quickly.

11

Do you know what each symbol is used for?

Practise writing the symbols on this page.

Andrew Brodie says...

Do you know what every symbol is?

\# is called a hash. People use it on Twitter!

\& is called an ampersand and is a quick way of writing 'and'.

Practise capital letters

It's important to write addresses very neatly.

Addresses do not have to be written in capital letters, but sometimes a complicated address is clearer when written in capitals. Try copying this address:

DR B K JOHNSON

FLAT #71B

HIGHER TOWER

469 KEWALRAM

SINGAPORE

S69974325

Write your own address in capital letters.

Now write your school address in capital letters.

Write the alphabet, using capital letters.

A B C D E F G H I J K L M N O P Q R S T U V W X Y Z

Write the alphabet again. Time yourself. How quickly can you write it?

Time taken, in seconds.

Try writing the alphabet again. Can you write it even more quickly and still keep it tidy?

Copy the addresses. Write each one in neat capital letters.

MISS S JENKINS
297 FORD STREET
VAUXHALL HILL
CARDIFF
CF29 3RT

PROFESSOR JANE GIBBS
17 PRIORY GARDENS
EDINBURGH
EH18 4DW

Practise slope joins

These letters are joined with a slope join.

au   *au*

Practise these words that have slope joins between their letters.

equal

quiet

quite

audio

audience

calculate

decimal

minimum

minimal

likely

mathematics

Which of these words are connected to maths?

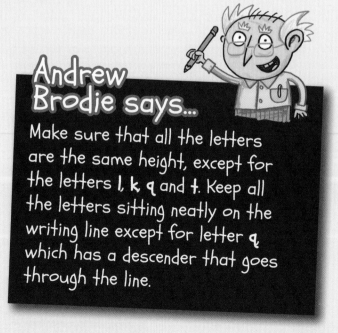

Andrew Brodie says...

Make sure that all the letters are the same height, except for the letters l, k, q and t. Keep all the letters sitting neatly on the writing line except for letter q which has a descender that goes through the line.

Practise bridge joins

Letters which finish at the top are joined to the next letter with a bridge join.

These letters are joined with a bridge join.

or   or

Practise these words that have some slope joins and some bridge joins.

reflector
junior
interior
doctor
calculator
adventure
adventurous
thermometer
temperature
nurse
operation

Which of these words relate to hospitals? Write them neatly below.

Andrew Brodie says...

Makes sure that all the letters are the same height, except for the letters with ascenders or descenders. Keep all the letters sitting neatly on the writing line.

Try joining letter b to a letter a. You need to finish the letter b then use a slope join from where the letter b ended.

band band

band band

Try these words, which use a joined letter b.

behaviour
billion
blending
binding

Do you want to join from a letter b or would you prefer not to? You can choose. You can also choose whether to join from a letter p. Try these words. Copy them exactly as they are shown.

repeated
prime
popular
population
perimeter
capacity

In this book, we have chosen to use the joining letter b and the joining letter p.

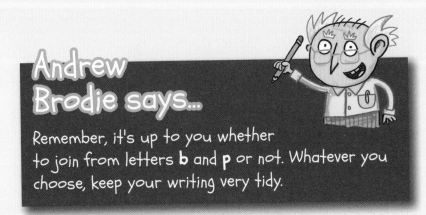

Andrew Brodie says...

Remember, it's up to you whether to join from letters **b** and **p** or not. Whatever you choose, keep your writing very tidy.

You can choose whether to join from letter **s** and letter **z** or not.

Try joining letter s to a letter o. You need to finish the letter s, then use a slope join from where the letter s ends.

soap soap

Try these words, which use a joined letter s.

sequence
square
sister
symbol
shallow
surface

Do you want to join from a letter s or would you prefer not to? You can also choose whether to join from letter z. Try these words. Copy them exactly as they are shown.

zebra
zero
lazy
crazy

In this book, we have chosen to use the joining letter s and the joining letter z.

Speedy work

See how quickly you can write!

Practise writing these words as quickly as possible. Time how long it takes you to write five copies of each one.

Time taken, in seconds.

appetite

prism

positive

because

sphere

spherical

trapezium

battery

batteries

parallel

Write each word five times.
Work as fast as you can but keep your writing tidy.

apples
application
bleeps
spears
mechanism
pentathlon
triplets
library
February

Time yourself. How quickly can you fill the apples? How quickly can you fill the pears?

apple

pear

Time taken, in seconds.

Time taken, in seconds.

Loopy letter g

Try writing letter g with a loop.

To loop or not to loop?

g g

g g

We can use the loop on the letter g to lead into a slope join. In that way, we can join g to letters that follow. Try these words that include the letter g. Write each word three times, really neatly.

graph
giraffe
range
diagram
bought
roughly
integer
negative
pictogram
percentage

Eight of the words above could be used in relation to maths. Write the words.

Andrew Brodie says...

Remember, you can choose whether to join from letter g or not. If you choose to join, you will need to use the looped letter g.

Loopy letter y

Try writing letter y with a loop.

y

y

We can use the loop on the letter y to lead into a slope join. In that way, we can join y to letters that follow. Try these words that include the letter y. Write each word three times, really neatly.

yellow
pyramid
cymbals
symbol
cylinder
recycle
symmetry
symmetrical
psychology
yacht

Five of the words above could be used in relation to maths. Write the words.

Andrew Brodie says...

In this book, we have chosen to use the looped letter y.

Loopy letter j

Try writing letter j with a loop.

We can use the loop on the letter j to lead into a slope join. In that way, we can join j to letters that follow. Try these words that include the letter j. Write each word three times, as neatly as you can.

judge

jury

judgement

major

majority

junior

juggle

juggling

justify

justification

jubilant

jubilee

jubilation

injure

injuries

Don't forget that you will need to dot the letter j after you have finished writing the word.

Andrew Brodie says...

In this book, we have chosen to use the looped letter j.

23

Loopy letter f

We don't need to use a looped letter **f**.

Try writing letter f with a loop.

We can use the loop on the letter f to lead into a slope join. In that way we can join f to letters that follow. Try these joins.

factor

fraction

Do you want to join from a letter f or would you prefer not to? Unlike letters g, y or j, you can choose to join from a letter f without using a loop by using the cross-bar instead.

fifth

twelfth

fiftieth

fifteenth

freezing

frozen

frequency

factorise

Which type of letter f do you prefer?

Andrew Brodie says...

In this book, we have chosen not to use the looped letter **f** but to join using the cross-bar instead.

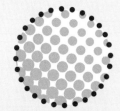

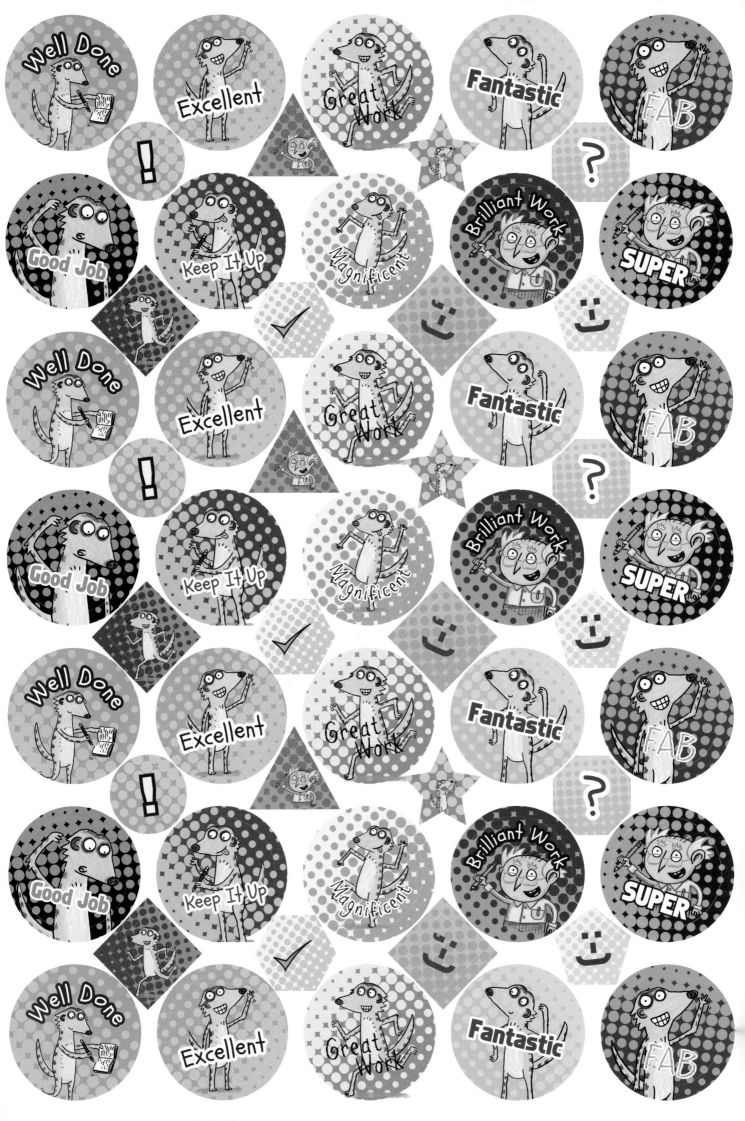

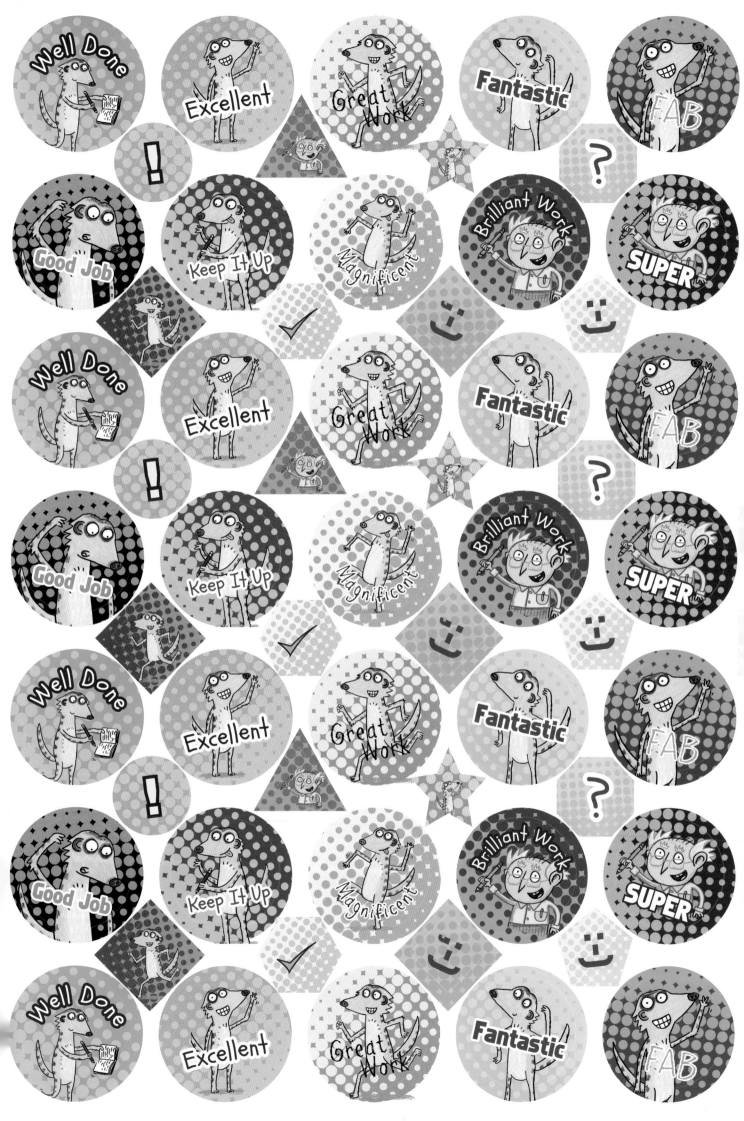

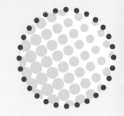

Practise loopy letters

Practise these sentences, which contain lots of looped letters.

We enjoyed eating jellies on the yellow yacht yesterday.

The gregarious girls were giggling with joy.

The judge asked the jury to act judiciously.

The boys in the group were learning to juggle jollily.

We regularly go cycling alongside the quay.

They generally rejoice joyfully when they get great goals.

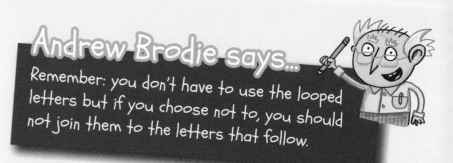

Andrew Brodie says...

Remember: you don't have to use the looped letters but if you choose not to, you should not join them to the letters that follow.

25

Write each word three times.
Work as fast as you can but keep your writing tidy.

length

height

eighty

eighth

percentages

negatively

symmetrical

enjoyment

enjoyably

hydrofoil

hydraulic

Write each word five times. Time yourself.
How quickly can you complete each set?

 **Time taken, in seconds.**

Sydney

Beijing

Tokyo

Write this sentence as neatly as you can:

The gaggle of geese were chased by some gulls.

Using punctuation

Punctuation should be as neat as the words.

We use speech marks to show when somebody is speaking. Speech marks are sometimes called inverted commas.

Copy these short pieces of speech exactly as they are written.

"Good morning everybody," said the headteacher.

"Good morning," replied the children.

"Today we are going to talk about yesterday's events," continued the headteacher. "It was a great sports' day and you should all be very proud."

Copy this short conversation.

"It's a perfect day today," said Davinder.
"But it may rain later," responded Will.
"So we'll make the most of it now," smiled Davinder.

Using question marks

Every question ends with a question mark.

Practise writing the question mark.

Copy these short conversations.

"What is the capital city of Scotland?"
asked the geography teacher.
"I think it's Edinburgh," replied Karl.

"Good, so what's the capital city of Wales?"
continued the teacher.
"Is it Swansea?" asked Karl.

"No, it's not Swansea," said the teacher.
"Does anybody else know?"
"It's Cardiff," said Grace.

Andrew Brodie says...

Don't forget to use your best handwriting.
Remember to start a new line when the speaker changes.

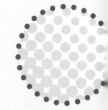

Using exclamation marks

Practise writing the exclamation mark.

!

!

Copy these short conversations.

"What is the name of a four-sided shape with opposite sides that are parallel?" asked the teacher.

"A rectangle!" called Izzy.

"That does have opposite sides that are parallel. What if the corners are not right angles?"

"It's a parallelogram!" shouted Rob eagerly.

"Don't call out, Robert!" said the teacher crossly.

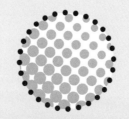

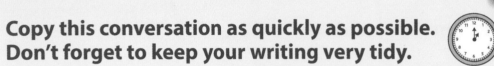

Another conversation

Can you write quickly but still keep your work tidy?

Copy this conversation as quickly as possible.
Don't forget to keep your writing very tidy.

"How many people are there in your class?"
asked Mum.
"I think there are twenty-seven," replied Laura.
"Do you want them all to come?"
"Is that ok?"
"Well, it's a lot of people, but they can come
if that's what you want."
"Thanks, Mum, that's great!"

Complete the conversation

I hope you can think of things to say!

Here is the start of a conversation.
Copy it out then try to add a few more lines.

"Do you want to come over to my place?" asked my friend.
"That would be great," I replied.

Andrew Brodie says...

Don't forget to start a new line when the speaker changes. Did you remember to write a comma, a question mark, an exclamation mark or a full stop before each set of closing speech marks?

Time yourself copying each short conversation.

"Where's the nearest library?" asked Izzy.
"It's near the park," replied Jez.
"So, where's the park?" asked Izzy.
"Next to the library!" said Jez unhelpfully.

Time taken, in seconds.

"Have you got any pets at home?" asked Jasdeep.
"Only seven," replied Ethan.
"Only seven! That sounds a lot to me!"
"Well, six of them are goldfish!"

Time taken, in seconds.

Write two more lines to add to this conversation.

"Where would you like to go on holiday?" asked Mum.
"When are we going?" Sam responded.

Useful rhymes

Copy the rhyme carefully.

Pentagons have five sides,
Hexagons have six.
Heptagons have seven sides,
So now what's in the mix?

Octagons have eight sides,
Nonagons have one more.
Decagons have ten you know,
And squares, they just have four!

Andrew Brodie says...

Make sure that all your handwriting is your very best.

Useful rhymes

Do you know how many days there are in each month?

Copy out the rhyme.

Thirty days has September,
April, June and November.
All the rest have thirty-one,
Except for February alone,
Which has twenty-eight days clear
And twenty-nine in each leap year.

Time yourself writing out the eight months of the year that are missing from the lines below. How quickly can you complete each line?

Time taken, in seconds.

January

April

July

October

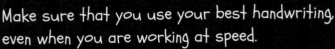

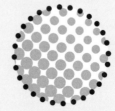

Useful rhymes

On this page and the next is a very old rhyme about parts of speech.

Copy the rhyme carefully.

Three little words we often see
Are ARTICLES – a, an and the.

A NOUN's the name of any thing,
A school, or garden, hoop, or swing.

ADJECTIVES tell the kind of noun,
As great, small, pretty, white or brown.

Instead of nouns the PRONOUNS stand –
John's head, his face, my arm, your hand.

VERBS tell of something being done –
To read, write, count, sing, jump or run.

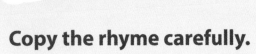

This is the second part of the rhyme about parts of speech.

Copy the rhyme carefully.

How things are done, the ADVERBS tell,
As slowly, quickly, ill or well.

A PREPOSITION stands before
A noun, as in or through a door.

CONJUNCTIONS join the words together,
As men and women, wind or weather.

The INTERJECTION shows surprise,
As Oh, how ugly! Ah, how weird!

The whole are called NINE PARTS OF SPEECH,
Which Reading, Writing, Speaking teach.

Andrew Brodie says...
Did you copy the capital letters perfectly?

Useful rhymes

Which planet is closest to the sun?

Copy the rhyme carefully.

The closest planet to the sun,
Is Mercury, a smallish one.

Next is Venus, then the Earth
Then it's Mars, what's it worth?

Jupiter is the biggest one,
Saturn's the sixth from the sun.

Uranus has twenty-seven moons
Thirteen moons are Neptune's.

Using clues from the rhyme, write the names of the planets in order of distance from the sun.

Andrew Brodie says...
Did you write the planets' names in your best handwriting?

Copy this rhyme very neatly.

One squared is one,
Two squared is three more.
Three squared is nine,
Sixteen's the square of four.

Five fives are twenty-five,
Six sixes are thirty-six,
Seven sevens are forty-nine.
I'm getting lots of ticks!

Eight eights are sixty-four,
Eighty-one's the square of nine,
One hundred is the square of ten,
That will do just fine.

Finished stories must be written in best handwriting.

Below is the start of a story. Copy the start then write some more of the story.

The plane slammed into the ground, then rolled over and over before coming to a shuddering halt. Jas climbed out of the cockpit carefully and, despite her dizziness, managed to check herself over.

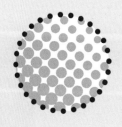

Don't forget the rules for writing conversations!

Here is the start of a conversation.
Copy it out, then add some more to finish it.

"What did you do that for?" asked Sim crossly.

"I didn't mean to do it, it was an accident!" replied Jo.

"Do you really expect me to believe that?"

"Yes, why not?"

"Because you keep causing trouble!" exclaimed Sim.

Andrew Brodie says...

Remember that speech marks go around the words spoken and that there is always a comma, an exclamation mark, a question mark or a full stop before the closing speech marks.

Writing poems

Remember: poems usually have a capital letter at the start of each line.

Copy the limerick carefully.

There was a young lady from Tring,
Who wanted to learn how to sing.
Her voice went so high,
That birds fell from the sky,
And her eyes popped out with a ping!

Use you best handwriting to copy the haiku poem.

The lark is rising,
Short bursts into the blue sky.
Tiny speck at height.

Try writing your own haiku poem.

Andrew Brodie says...

Most haiku poems have three lines. They often have five syllables in the first line, seven in the second line and five syllables in the last line.

Play script

**Copy the start of a play script about a chance meeting.
Write some extra lines at the end to finish the script.**

Saffie: Watch where you're going!

Harry: Sorry, it was an accident. Are you ok?

Saffie: No, not really. I'll probably get a black eye after that!

Harry: Look, I said I was sorry. I don't think you're hurt that badly, are you?

Andrew Brodie says...

Remember that you don't need to use speech marks in play scripts but you do need to start a new line when the speaker changes.

Handwriting tips

Copy out these tips in your very best handwriting.

Most letters should sit neatly on the writing line.

Letters with descenders should pass through the writing line.

Most letters should join to the letters that follow them.

Punctuation marks should be written in the right places.

Neat handwriting looks really good and is much easier for people to read.

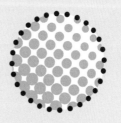

The rhyme below is actually part of a play script. It comes from 'Macbeth' by William Shakespeare. It is spoken by one of the three witches, who is mixing various unpleasant ingredients in her cauldron. Copy it out using your best handwriting.

Fillet of a fenny snake,
In the cauldron boil and bake;
Eye of newt and toe of frog,
Wool of bat and tongue of dog,
Adder's fork and blind-worm's sting,
Lizard's leg and howlet's wing,
For a charm of powerful trouble,
Like a hell-broth boil and bubble.

ANSWERS

Talk about the progress checks with your child, encouraging him/her to match each one with the copies shown here.

Andrew Brodie says...

Check the following:

- Does your child remember to make the tall letters taller than the other letters?
- Do the letters sit neatly on the writing lines?
- Do the letters such as g, p and y go through the line?
- Is letter j written correctly? Does it go through the line? Has it got a dot, like a letter i?
- Are most of the letters joined?
- Has your child made a consistent decision about whether or not to use loops with letters g, p and y?

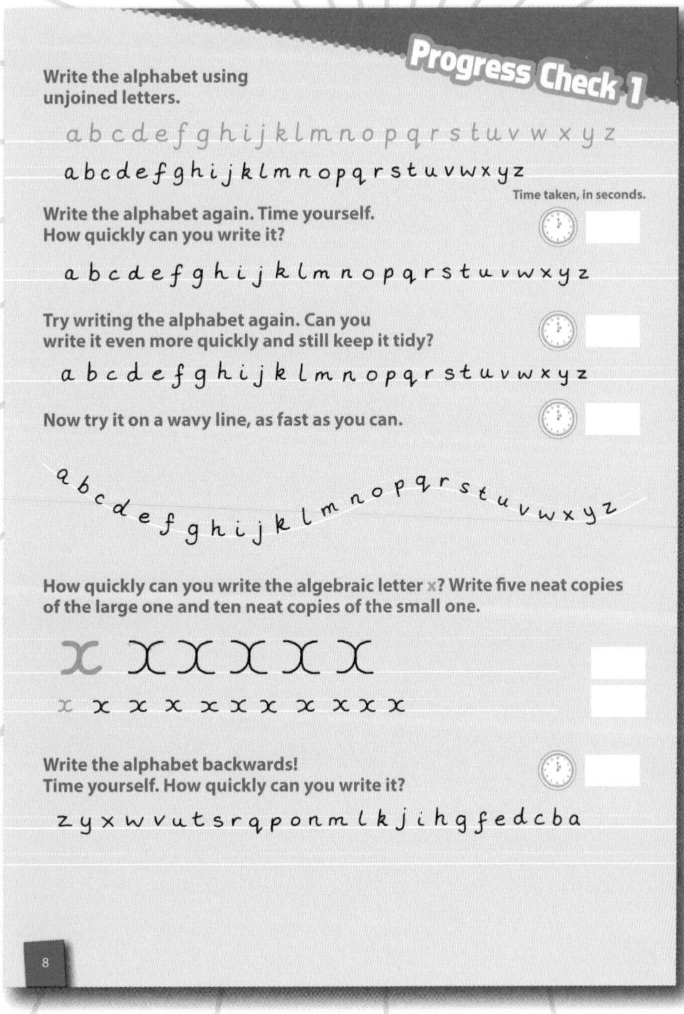

Progress Check 1

Write the alphabet using unjoined letters.

abcdefghijklmnopqrstuvwxyz

abcdefghijklmnopqrstuvwxyz

Write the alphabet again. Time yourself. How quickly can you write it?

Time taken, in seconds.

abcdefghijklmnopqrstuvwxyz

Try writing the alphabet again. Can you write it even more quickly and still keep it tidy?

abcdefghijklmnopqrstuvwxyz

Now try it on a wavy line, as fast as you can.

abcdefghijklmnopqrstuvwxyz

How quickly can you write the algebraic letter x? Write five neat copies of the large one and ten neat copies of the small one.

x X X X X X

x x x x x x x x x x

Write the alphabet backwards! Time yourself. How quickly can you write it?

zyxwvutsrqponmlkjihgfedcba

8

Write the alphabet, using capital letters.

A B C D E F G H I J K L M N O P Q R S T U V W X Y Z

A B C D E F G H I J K L M N O P Q R S T U V W X Y Z

Write the alphabet again. Time yourself. How quickly can you write it?

Time taken, in seconds.

A B C D E F G H I J K L M N O P Q R S T U V W X Y Z

Try writing the alphabet again. Can you write it even more quickly and still keep it tidy?

A B C D E F G H I J K L M N O P Q R S T U V W X Y Z

Copy the addresses. Write each one in neat capital letters.

MISS S JENKINS
297 FORD STREET
VAUXHALL HILL
CARDIFF
CF29 3RT

MISS S JENKINS
297 FORD STREET
VAUXHALL HILL
CARDIFF
CF29 3RT

PROFESSOR JANE GIBBS
17 PRIORY GARDENS
EDINBURGH
EH18 4DW

PROFESSOR JANE GIBBS
17 PRIORY GARDENS
EDINBURGH
EH18 4DW

14

Write each word five times. Work as fast as you can but keep your writing tidy.

apples   apples
application   application
bleeps   bleeps
spears   spears
mechanism   mechanism
pentathlon   pentathlon
triplets   triplets
library   library
February   February

Time yourself. How quickly can you fill the apples? How quickly can you fill the pears?

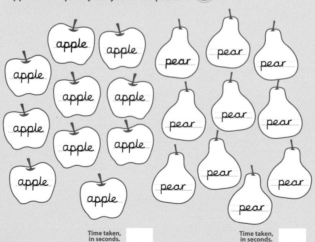

Time taken, in seconds.

Time taken, in seconds.

20

46

Write each word three times.
Work as fast as you can but keep your writing tidy.

length   length   length   length
height   height   height   height
eighty   eighty   eighty   eighty
eighth   eighth   eighth   eighth
percentages   percentages   percentages   percentages
negatively   negatively   negatively   negatively
symmetrical   symmetrical   symmetrical   symmetrical
enjoyment   enjoyment   enjoyment   enjoyment
enjoyably   enjoyably   enjoyably   enjoyably
hydrofoil   hydrofoil   hydrofoil   hydrofoil
hydraulic   hydraulic   hydraulic   hydraulic

Write each word five times. Time yourself.   Time taken, in seconds.
How quickly can you complete each set?

Sydney   Sydney   Sydney   Sydney   Sydney   Sydney

Beijing   Beijing   Beijing   Beijing   Beijing   Beijing

Tokyo   Tokyo   Tokyo   Tokyo   Tokyo   Tokyo

Write this sentence as neatly as you can:

The gaggle of geese were chased by some gulls.

The gaggle of geese were chased by some gulls.

26

Time yourself copying each short conversation.

"Where's the nearest library?" asked Izzy.
"It's near the park," replied Jez.
"So, where's the park?" asked Izzy.
"Next to the library!" said Jez unhelpfully.

"Where's the nearest library?" asked Izzy.
"It's near the park," replied Jez.
"So, where's the park?" asked Izzy.
"Next to the library!" said Jez unhelpfully.

Time taken, in seconds.

"Have you got any pets at home?" asked Jasdeep.
"Only seven," replied Ethan.
"Only seven! That sounds a lot to me!"
"Well, six of them are goldfish!"

"Have you got any pets at home?" asked Jasdeep.
"Only seven," replied Ethan.
"Only seven! That sounds a lot to me!"
"Well, six of them are goldfish!"

Time taken, in seconds.

Write two more lines to add to this conversation.

"Where would you like to go on holiday?" asked Mum.
"When are we going?" Sam responded.

"As soon as you finish school for the summer" said Mum.
"I can't wait!" exclaimed Sam, grinning.

32

Copy this rhyme very neatly.

One squared is one,
Two squared is three more.
Three squared is nine,
Sixteen's the square of four.
One squared is one,
Two squared is four.
Three squared is nine,
Sixteen's the square of four.

Five fives are twenty-five,
Six sixes are thirty-six,
Seven sevens are forty-nine.
I'm getting lots of ticks!
Five fives are twenty-five,
Six sixes are thirty-six,
Seven sevens are forty-nine.
I'm getting lots of ticks.

Eight eights are sixty-four,
Eighty-one's the square of nine,
One hundred is the square of ten,
That will do just fine.
Eight eights are sixty-four,
Eighty-one's the square of nine,
One hundred is the square of ten,
That will do just fine.

The rhyme below is actually part of a play
script. It comes from 'Macbeth' by William Shakespeare.
It is spoken by one of the three witches, who is mixing various
unpleasant ingredients in her cauldron. Copy it out using your best
handwriting.

Fillet of a fenny snake,
In the cauldron boil and bake;
Eye of newt and toe of frog,
Wool of bat and tongue of dog,
Adder's fork and blind-worm's sting,
Lizard's leg and howlet's wing,
For a charm of powerful trouble,
Like a hell-broth boil and bubble.

Fillet of a fenny snake,
In the cauldron boil and bake;
Eye of newt and toe of frog,
Wool of bat and tongue of dog,
Adder's fork and blind-worm's sting
Lizard's leg and howlet's wing,
For a charm of powerful trouble,
Like a hell broth boil and bubble.